# PLACES

Röble

PLACES

Röble

Copyright © 2024 Röble
All rights reserved. No part of this book may be reproduced, stored in a retrieval system, or transmitted in any form or by any means, electronic, mechanical, photocopying, recording, or otherwise, without the prior written permission of the author.

Published by Röble Publishing
Printed in U.S.A

ISBN: 978-1-7354239-0-6

Cover Design by Dillon Sturtevant
Edited by H.E. Boyer

A sore spot in the mouth yearns to be pressed
You are unsure whether pressing it
is somehow healing

Dedicated to my friends,

for being a part of this journey with me
for helping me survive my first heartbreak

I didn't know there would be so many more

M,

You were one of the best and worst things to ever happen to me....

And I would do it all over again

I. SWEET BEGINNINGS

Classroom
Park Bench
Parking Garage
Couch
Doorway
Your Bed
Your Apartment Part I
Community Garden
Hospital
Restaurant Part I

II. SWEET ENDINGS

Your Apartment Part II
St Thomas
Ferry
School
Backyard
My Bed
Kitchen Floor
Restaurant Part II

III. SWEET NOTHINGS

Driveway
Payphone
Everyplace

I. SWEET BEGINNINGS.

## CLASSROOM

I had spent so much time with these black counters
A cool surface to touch on a warm Seattle day
3 stories up and 3 floors of stories
Memories of cells, plants and dissected animals

You walked into the room
soft bristly face
The ever-present cliché "love at first sight" rings true
Should have known then
it was "lust at first sight"
You would ruin all Scorpio men for me one day

Still caught in your trance
Lab comes next week
Scanning around
at the sea of black counters
Acting as If I had not already chosen my seat

The one next to you.

The funny thing about anatomy
It's the perfect catalyst to touch
Friendly pokes as I tried to find your hip bone,
That elusive and tempting iliac crest,
A friendly grab of the hand as you pull me away,
"play it cool" comes to my head

From this meeting to now, it's all a blur
Anatomy was ours
First meeting in a day
You'd come here from work
and I from home
Hands met under the table
Your warmth met mine

# PARK BENCH

It was on this bench
We shared our very first kiss
That cool summer night

Anatomy class
Where I first laid eyes on you
That bristly face

The past and present
Foretold desires come true
I melt in your lips

PARKING GARAGE

Level 3
Lights flicker,
Buzz.
Pinned against the concrete pillar
Cold on my back
Swift grab by the collar and I pull you in
Warmth is only 15 feet away, the door of your apartment seemingly within reach.
You pull away,

You've always said you hate being affectionate in public…

Gentle lips are all it takes.
And it's clear you're not going anywhere
I pull you closer
I don't care who sees

Wet kisses
Raw face

Now you don't care who sees.

COUCH

1-part mushrooms
1-part love
2-parts desire
1-tablespoon of reality
2 cups of release
Pinch of imagination

1. In a large bowl mix 1 part mushrooms and 1 part love. Let rest for 30 minutes.
2. Take your 2 parts desire and migrate to the couch. Soft kisses on the lip, soft kisses on the neck.
3. Simmer.
4. Melt into the couch. All sensations felt simultaneously. Heat and sound amplified. Roaring breaths in your ear.
5. When the visual representations appear, and touch is overwhelming, it's time to add 2 cups of release and bring to a rolling boil.
6. Mix sparingly until you have surrendered to desire, vulnerability and passion. (Note this may take a while).
7. Take your 1 tablespoon of reality and throw it out the window.
8. Close your eyes and add a pinch of imagination.

## DOORWAY

You were home
Making me dinner


Irises are your favorite,
And I've got them with me.
Blue with centers tinged gold
I knock, though I don't need to
You arrive
Your face glistens with sweat
Clues of your efforts
Slight exasperation
Homemaker you are not
A smirk gives me away

Warmth flushes my face
Your hand cradles my chin
Kiss at the door
Flowers in hand
Frozen in time
Noses locked
Stubbly face
Foreheads touch

YOUR BED

Your sweet nothings whispered in my ear

"I would marry you and you would not have to work"
"We would have a cute house, and you would stay home and garden and cook"
"Little Patricks and Chéitos would be running in the yard"

"I would love that."

## YOUR APARTMENT PART I

I feel you move
Slowly, deliberately
You don't want to wake me.

Like children who feign slumber
I keep my eyes closed

Small moments pass,
Silence is broken
The blades grind away
Scent wafts near me
Fresh coffee beans
With dark earthy tones
Smells travel so fast
In this tiny place.

Shower runs
My eyes still closed

I lay there knowing
I should probably get up
I stare at the ceiling
Water stops
Rustling of towels
Your steps ever closer.
Smelling of soap
You give me a kiss
One on the cheek,
The way you look into my eyes,
Your dark pools of honey
They seem to stare beyond,
In the place I imagine my soul lives
And one on the lips

I want you to always love me this much

With a sly tender smile
A hand reveals
The warm gift
A mug full of coffee

## COMMUNITY GARDEN

It was a lovely afternoon. Both without obligation and worry, we visit your plot.

Much work to do as spring approaches.

A trellis from your mother goes in, and peas are planted around it.

You're so cute getting dirty, my big strong man, half complaining the whole time. You tell me the story about how you got this plot and the older ladies who gave you orientation. We laughed about their attachment to memory and leaving those things that have come from years prior. In this case, a rose bush in the corner of your plot.

---

I was recently there, that plot now someone else's, but the rosebush is still there. Outlived and outgrown even us, whatever us is.

---

Later that season we went back to garden,
and picked from the things growing there.

Dinner is made in your tiny kitchen
My hands made busy with garden spoils

A large nasturtium leaf forms the perfect container
Tidbits and small ingredients
 a little pepper, some shrimp, just a dab of honey

All wrapped tight I tell you "open wide"
You obey and then your face tightens into alarm

Garbled sounds and what I can only interpret as "what is it?"

"do you trust me?"

Chuckles and hearty laughs as your face melts into delight

HOSPITAL

–You told me that your other boys would never come visit you
– "Well, I'm not like your other boys– I declare mischievously
–No, no you are not– a smile forming at the corners of your mouth

We've talked about those other boys many times
How infatuated and out of control they get
Driven mad by your passion
Unable to tame or control you.

I, for whatever reason, seem to be the exception
Able to listen, help and redirect.
You seem to always be in crisis
And working where I did
Moving from one crisis to another,
Just a simple and familiar transition
Done without consciousness...

Where were we?
Ah yes, lunch time at the hospital.

I can't remember what I brought you for lunch
But I remember you liking it
We teased across the table

The way you look at me with that devilish smile
I smile knowing the dimples that rarely make an appearance are well in sight
It was the way you looked at me right before we kissed.

As we sat there in that unassuming cafeteria
Everyone wrapped in scrubs, grabbing lunch

But no one here knew who we were
And what you did with your other boys
With me.
There was nowhere to steal a kiss

Forbidden even to hold hands across the table
Embrace nowhere in sight

## RESTAURANT PART I

I can't remember what you said,
Or what I said,

White fragility and brown anger fill the air
Hushed words said pointedly, meant to poke, stab and wound.
Back and force across the table.

We became the couple arguing quietly.
A glass comes down.
Silverware clutched like pearls.

The waitress comes, feigned smiles, and orders placed.
"everything is great thanks"
"yes, more water would be lovely"

Our food comes.
I walk out of the restaurant.--
A whole new meaning to a "breath of fresh air"
Wrapped in a pea coat my body is blistering.
Gasping for the coolness that seems so hard to catch

Why did I not keep walking?
I stood there waiting for you, the world silent.
I stood there waiting for you, wrapped in fury
Rain drops evaporating as they hit my skin
Eventually the fire blows out.

You walk out of the restaurant.
Knowing I overreacted, (Did I though?)
We always make up anyways
You hug me and I burst into tears.
"Come back inside, your food's getting cold"

## II. SWEET ENDINGS

## YOUR APARTMENT PART II

It was too early for me to be there. As starts every story about infidelity. Here I was anyways. I had no idea what I would find. There's your foreshadowing.

We had spent the night in separate beds.
I don't remember where I was coming from...

I walked up the stairs to your apartment. You were leaving for St. Thomas in about a week. These red carpeted stairs would become a thing of the past. Halfway up I stop at the west window. The rose garden abloom and yellow rue flowers emerge from the neighbor's yard.

I take my keys and turn the handle. No one home. Belongings all in multiple stages of packing. (Sigh) I need some water and a bit of coffee.

I walk over to your side of the bed, as if drawn there. Not looking for anything. Not wanting to find anything. A new package of condoms and open lube I have never seen before, and certainly not ours. A torn wrapper sits on the floor.

Before that moment, I had never known what the expression "you feel your heart sink" meant. Here I was feeling it. No anger. No disbelief. Just. Profound. Hurt. I lay down on the bed too tired to care who was in it and what happened. I fell asleep.

------

Hours later you come home. I hear the keys entering and I slowly start to wake.
What it must look like to you is that I came home and had lain down on my side as I always do.
The paraphernalia of your night still untouched and seemingly out of site from me.
I don't move.

You walk to your side of the bed, I feel you pulling the blanket, and pushing your shit under the bed.
Hurt turns to anger.

" I already saw it, I know who you were with last night"

A pause and then you grab me, as if to apologize. I don't know what to feel. My gaze turned away and I look past the wall. Your hand finds my chin, ready to turn my face and kiss me. I pull away feeling possessive, jealous and disgusted.

I forgave you though,
Love makes you do foolish things.

ST THOMAS

You were so far away
And I missed you so much.

Your schedule was so chaotic it seemed,
It was near impossible for me to try and find a time to visit.
I imagined what it would it be like to visit you in St. Thomas

I thought about my first trip to Puerto Rico
It was the very first time I had taken a trip on my own
I nearly had a panic attack just arriving in the airport

But here, I would be coming to you.
Searching for you as a familiar face in the airport terminal
The air would be warm and have a familiar saltiness

And just like that very first day in anatomy class
I know I would kiss you.
Knowing that we couldn't be who we were in public
sexual desire and tension would rise all the way to the car

Every single accidental touch, enough to send us wild.
And once in the car. It would take a momentary glance and
we'd both let loose to carnal instincts

Our very first lovemaking in a strange city would be endless,
You would come too quickly and that would be fine
But you always made sure to take care of me too

I'd be ready for more, and maybe this time I might get up to 3 rounds out of you.
But if not, I know that I would get all the kissing I wanted.
I'd ask you to put a hickey right under my collarbone.
I'd put one on your inner left thigh

— — —

But it was all a dream
I never got to go
I didn't get the coral beaches
Or the kisses
You had already spent the night with this man
I didn't understand the things that went through your mind

You said you didn't want to hurt me
But there was a nurse that you slept with
And now you were moving to the same complex where they lived

I asked you why you would do that
If you truly wanted to not hurt me
Why then, would you put yourself in the way of temptation

I can't even remember what you said to me
And now it doesn't even matter

FERRY

You were in St Thomas. Driving around in your rented car paid for by the agency that had contracted you there. You found yourself in an accident with a local. They were never on your side. Here you were a white man trapped in world of people of color. You had to play by their rules.

I tried to make you see the lighter side of things. That you, at the end of the day, would be able to leave that island you found so wretched. That while there were injustices at play you had means, privilege and power. You have parents who love you, and while you are able to, you have a loving mother who would pay for your accident.

White privilege and brown anger fill the air.

SCHOOL

I walked out of class
Spent the day texting
Like I do now with you, far away

Knowing you're with others,
Knowing you love attention,
Knowing you're insatiable,

You slept with him
You finally admitted,
But I didn't even have to ask you
Battling with feelings of possession,
You were not mine,
Battling with feelings of possession,
I was not yours

Watery eyes, began to feel commonplace and familiar.
Yet they offered no warmth,
I sat there on the second story and saw the beauty before me
A gorgeous sunset painted the horizon with peach and rose hues
But so engrossed, and attentive to you, to fixing you
Familiar words came to mind
Victor and his creation as he works hard to bring to light from darkness

"while I was thus engaged, heart and soul, in one pursuit. It was the most beautiful season… but my eyes were insensible to the charms of nature."

I would not be able to finish this class.
My friend comes out to greet me
He offers simple instructions,

Tell your story
A thousand times, and then twice more

His love had done the same
The hurt and pain we all go through
I'm offered a fortune

One day,
though I can't see it now, I would understand

I took that class 3 times

BACKYARD

Words never said to you

I talked to my friend today

He said "No."
No to you
No to us

It came so swiftly
Decisive, and sharp

"No."

My friend
He never says "No" to me
That should mean something…

I love you so much
But, this "No."
It stays with me
I want nothing more than to welcome you back
To melt in your arms
Melt in your lips

But…
I trust him.
More than I trust you.

MY BED

You came back to see me.
We are laying there in my bed, the small one
I took from you before you moved away.

A long awaited and planned trip
It was November; your birthday had just passed.
You'd be coming back in January, you started to say.
We could take a break now,
And be together then
You had started looking at where we might live

"Have you thought about us not being together anymore"

--
Before this day I had already made a plan.
He had as well.
--

"Oh, this wasn't about us being together"

After all the hurt how could I be here?
And in words I did know or could not articulate then.
I knew my self-worth
How could I endure the freedom you took with others
While I was locked away here?

We laid in bed
Holding each other
Time passes
"I thought we would be having sex by now"
I grinned- knowing the same thing

## KITCHEN FLOOR

You know...
There is nothing more sobering
Than crying on your kitchen floor
Listening to Adele,
And in one afternoon you might as well have written them
Every lyric becomes habit

Once the moment is over
Your melodramatic novela
You decide it's not enough

So you call your friend and make the drive over.
When he asks you what's wrong
You say,
"I've got a broken heart"
And immediately burst into more tears
Instant pity, and an embrace that tells they've been here before

But no, that's not enough,
You also need some comic relief
And your other friend arrives shortly

So you say the same thing to him
The saga's played itself through
You both burst out laughing
And more tears come
And as you sit in your friend's embrace
Staring at the ceiling together
For the first time in a while
You don't think of him

This warmth
Is mine

## RESTAURANT PART II

It seemed we were fine,
At least that's what we said.
Little did I know that I was just fooling myself.
It was the night where you realized how different we were, you even said to me, that's why we would have never worked out, you talked about how we were too different. We did fight a lot, that's true.

–"Oh, is that why? It certainly wasn't because of your other boys"
–"I forgot that I did that"
–"I didn't."

We had talked about being friends
And for once you even let me pay for my check
I hugged you,
And you kissed me on the cheek
You gave me your card, so I could stay in touch with you

I had blocked you on every platform I could–
And had made you so upset you did the same–
I got you there by doing things I'm not proud of.
But I take a slight satisfaction in doing something your other boys could never.
The moment that led up to this meeting was pure chance,
And of course I never forget a phone number.

It was a cool night,
As I drove home, through my familiar city,
I rolled down the window and cast your card out
I didn't want to need you anymore.

# III. SWEET NOTHINGS

DRIVEWAY

It was 2 weeks before I would move out of Seattle, and 4 years since I had spoken to you last.
And as if the universe had found some last way to try and keep me here,
You popped into my life by way of a friend,

Immediately my face flushes with warmth
And I long for you just like that first day
I know now what you said to my friend,

That you let a good one go
That you miss me
That you feel there's unfinished business

I do too....


Some things are better left unfinished.
I'd very much like to never see you again.

There is a part of me that will always love you
And I know there's a part of you that will always love me

Goodbye.

PAYPHONE

I really never forget a number

As I made the road trip down
Those thousand miles
Quarters burn heavy in my jeans

Every stop I would look for a payphone
Rather than risk calling from mine
96 miles before my new home and in the middle of nowhere

The quarters go in…
I wait for the prompts…
My shaking fingers dial…
The phone rings…
(I hold my breath)

Voicemail….
And it's not yours…
(sigh)

## EVERYPLACE

Everyplace.
Reminds me of you.
Of us.

Everyplace.
Haunts.

Everyplace
Changes
Memories
People

Everyplace
Forgets
You

I
Forget
You

I forgive you...

I forgive me.

www.ingramcontent.com/pod-product-compliance
Lightning Source LLC
Chambersburg PA
CBHW040311050426
42449CB00019B/3484